This book belongs to

_____

_____

To all the kids who like cookies
and animals.

Econ for Kids
Visit us on the web! www.econforkids.com
ISBN 978-0-57883-477-1 (paperback)
ISBN 978-1-954945-00-5 (hardcover)
ISBN 978-1-954945-12-8 (ebook)

What Is Money?

Kelly Lee

Charlie the bunny loves baking cookies.

He sells his delicious cookies for money.

What is money?

Money can be used to buy things

or to pay someone to do something for you.

Where does money come from?

Money does not fall from the sky.

Money does not grow on trees.

Charlie earns money from his
bakery business,

from helping out with extra chores,

 Helping out with the chores should be every family member's duty. Charlie earns money by doing extra chores.

and from selling used books.

Money can be earned at a job, such as a teacher,

a chef,

a doctor,

a scientist,

or an astronaut!

What does Charlie do with his money?

He puts it in 3 piggy banks.

 A bank is a safe place where people can store their money.

The first one is for spending.

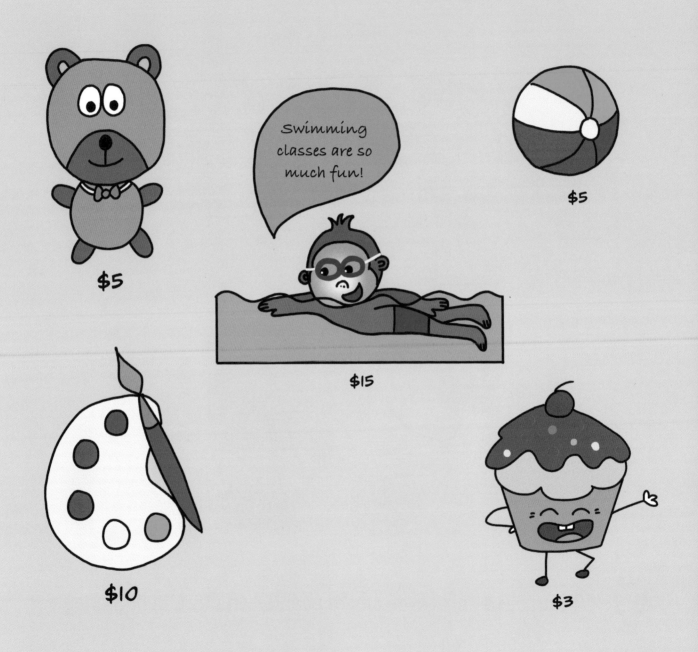

The second one is for sharing.

The third one is for saving.

Why save?

So that in the future, he can buy something really cool.

$80

$500

$50

What should he do?

?

$80

$50
IN SAVINGS

?

$50

?

He does not have enough money to buy both.

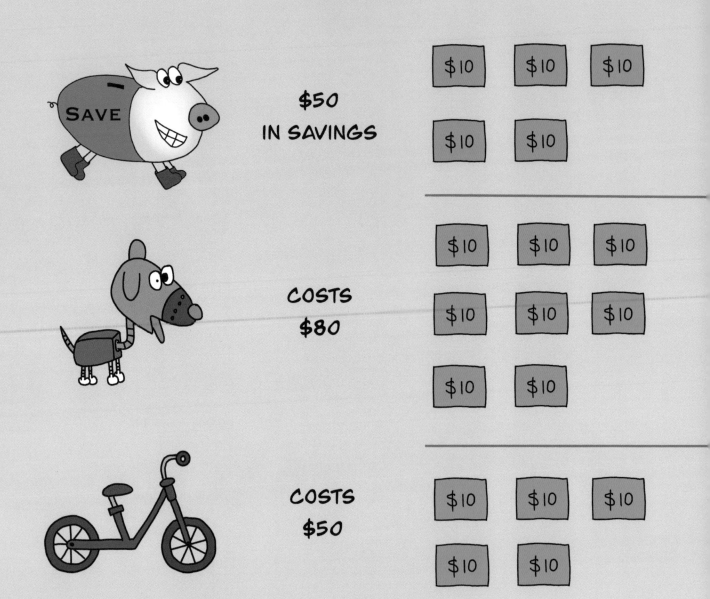

$50 IN SAVINGS — $10, $10, $10, $10, $10

COSTS $80 — $10, $10, $10, $10, $10, $10, $10, $10

COSTS $50 — $10, $10, $10, $10, $10

He needs to make a plan.

 See "How To Spend Wisely" in the same series for more explanation on planning.

Charlie keeps adding money to his "save" piggy bank. That piggy bank grows bigger and bigger!

$50 NOW $100 NEXT YEAR

Charlie is proud of his good money habits.

What is YOUR plan?

The End

Dear Parent/Grandparent/Caregiver,

Congratulations on giving your child a head start on their money management journey! Here are some fun activities you can do with them:

- Get 3 piggy banks or clear jars. There are also piggy banks that have 3 compartments (spend, share, save).

- Show your child different kinds of coins and bills.

- Teach them how to count money, perhaps using play money.

- Explain what you and other family members do to earn money (e.g., Auntie Lily is a teacher).

- Talk about the cost of items they see around them. For example, say, "This bag of oranges costs $5." Then, show them a $5 bill, and that five $1 bills are also worth $5.

- Encourage your child to use the money from their piggy bank to buy something, take them to the store, count the money in front of them, have them physically hand the money to the cashier, and count how much change is given.

- You may want to introduce other forms of money such as credit card and debit card.

- Give your child suggestions if they want to buy something that costs more than what they have (e.g., they can seek opportunities to earn money and/or wait for their next allowance).

- Talk to your child about how they can earn their own money (e.g., they can participate in a yard sale, or do extra chores around the house such as cleaning their baby sibling's room in addition to their own).

For any questions, suggestions, or any other finance topics you would like to see, please email kelly@econforkids.com. Thanks!

kelly Lee

Finance for Kids Books

 What Is Money?

 What Is a Credit Card?

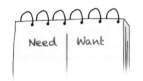 How to Spend Wisely

 What Is Supply and Demand?

Visit us at: www.econforkids.com

Printed in Great Britain
by Amazon

18140568R00020